AF409357

Capturing Reality in the Fascinating World of Photogrammetry

Writer: A. Scholtens

Cover design: A. Scholtens

© A. Scholtens

March 2023

Preface

Photogrammetry is a field that has been around for centuries, but it has taken a big leap forward in recent years thanks to the advancement of technology. With the introduction of digital cameras, drones and advanced software, photogrammetry has become a powerful tool for capturing reality in a way that was not possible before.

The book you hold in your hands, "Capturing Reality in the Fascinating World of Photogrammetry", is an informative guide for anyone wanting to learn more about the field of photogrammetry. The purpose of this book is to provide the reader with an understanding of the fundamental concepts of photogrammetry, its application, and its importance in various industries.

This book breaks down complex topics into easy-to-understand language. The chapters are arranged logically and follow a clear and concise structure. The book provides a comprehensive overview of photogrammetry, including its history, principles, and the tools and software used for data processing. It also explores the application of photogrammetry in various fields such as architecture, engineering, surveying and archaeology.

The book not only covers the theoretical aspects of photogrammetry, but also provides practical examples and case studies. These examples have been carefully selected to illustrate the application of photogrammetry in real-life scenarios.

I would like to point out to the reader that this field changes quickly and that it is therefore possible that information in this book will no longer be completely up-to-date at some point.

Regardless, this book is an invaluable resource that will broaden your knowledge and understanding of photogrammetry.

I hope you will enjoy reading it.

A. Scholtens

Table of Contents

Chapter 1: Introduction to Photogrammetry

Photogrammetry is a technique that uses photographs to gather and analyze spatial data, allowing us to create maps, models, and other visual representations of the world around us. It has a rich history dating back over a century, and has been used for a wide variety of purposes, from surveying and mapping to architectural documentation and environmental monitoring. In recent years, photogrammetry has become an increasingly important tool for understanding and managing the world, and it has never been more accessible or user-friendly.

1.1 Definition of Photogrammetry

Photogrammetry is a scientific discipline that uses photographs to measure and understand the physical world. It is based on the principle that photographs contain a wealth of information about the objects and features that are captured within them. Photogrammetry uses mathematical algorithms and computer software to extract this information and transform it into maps, models, and other visual representations of the world.

1.2 The History of Photogrammetry

Photogrammetry has its roots in the mid-19th century, when it was first used as a tool for surveying and mapping. Early photogrammetrists used simple equipment, such as a camera and a ruler, to measure the size and shape of objects in photographs. Over time, as cameras and other equipment became more sophisticated, photogrammetry evolved into a more complex and powerful discipline, capable of producing high-precision maps and models.

In the 20th century, photogrammetry was used for a wide variety of purposes, including architectural documentation, land use planning, and environmental monitoring. With the advent of aerial photography and satellite imagery, photogrammetry became an indispensable tool for understanding the world from above. Today, photogrammetry continues to evolve, and new technologies, such as unmanned aerial vehicles (UAVs) or drones, have made it more accessible and user-friendly than ever before.

1.3 Contemporary Applications of Photogrammetry

Photogrammetry is used in a wide variety of fields today, from agriculture and archaeology to engineering and environmental science. Some of the most exciting and innovative applications of photogrammetry in recent years include:

- **Disaster management and emergency response:**

    Photogrammetry is used to map the impact of natural disasters, such as hurricanes, earthquakes, and wildfires, in real-time. It is also used to assess the damage caused by these events and to help plan recovery efforts.

- **Environmental monitoring and assessment:**

Photogrammetry is used to monitor the health of ecosystems, such as forests and wetlands, and to assess the impact of human activities, such as deforestation and urbanization, on the environment.

- **Cultural heritage and archaeology:**

Photogrammetry is used to document and preserve cultural heritage sites, such as ancient ruins and historic buildings. It is also used to study and understand the cultural and historical context of these sites.

- **Urban planning and development:**

Photogrammetry is used to plan and manage urban development, including the design and construction of roads, bridges, and buildings.

We will discuss all of these topics in detail in this book.

1.4 The Future of Photogrammetry

Photogrammetry is constantly evolving and adapting to new technologies and applications. In recent years, the rapid advancement of unmanned aerial vehicles (UAVs), or drones, has revolutionized the field of photogrammetry, making it more accessible, user-friendly, and cost-effective than ever before.

One of the key trends in the future of photogrammetry is the integration of photogrammetry with other technologies, such as artificial intelligence

(AI) and machine learning (ML). This will allow photogrammetrists to automate many of the manual processes involved in image analysis, making photogrammetry faster, more efficient, and more accurate.

Another important trend is the use of photogrammetry in virtual and augmented reality (VR and AR) applications. Photogrammetry can be used to create 3D models of real-world objects and environments, which can then be used in VR and AR experiences. This has the potential to revolutionize fields such as gaming, education, and tourism.

In addition, photogrammetry will continue to play an important role in environmental monitoring and assessment, as well as in the management of natural resources, such as forests and water resources. It will also be used to study and monitor the effects of climate change, such as rising sea levels and changing weather patterns, and to help plan and implement adaptation and mitigation strategies.

Overall, the future of photogrammetry is bright, and it will continue to play a critical role in our understanding and management of the world around us. As new technologies emerge and new applications are developed, photogrammetry will continue to evolve and adapt, and it will remain an essential tool for understanding and managing the physical world.

Chapter 2: Where to place Photogrammetry

Photogrammetry is a scientific discipline that uses photographs to measure and understand the physical world. It is based on the principle that photographs contain a wealth of information about the objects and features that are captured within them. Photogrammetry uses mathematical algorithms and computer software to extract this information and transform it into maps, models, and other visual representations of the world.

2.1 Basic Principles of Photogrammetry

In this chapter we describe the basic principles of photogrammetry.

2.1.1 Object-to-image

The process of converting the physical world into an image is known as object-to-image. This is the first and crucial step in photogrammetry as it lays the foundation for the rest of the photogrammetric process.

The objective of object-to-image is to capture the details and features of the physical world in a 2D image format that can be processed and analyzed using photogrammetric techniques. This is typically done using a camera, which is equipped with a lens that captures the light reflected off the objects in the physical world.

The camera captures an image of the object and records it in a digital format that can be processed using photogrammetry software. The image captured by the camera is then transformed into a digital representation of the object, including its shape, size, and position in space.

In recent years, advancements in technology have allowed photogrammetrists to use other imaging technologies, such as laser scanners, to capture images of the physical world. These laser scanners emit pulses of light that bounce off the objects in the physical world and are captured by the scanner, creating a 3D representation of the object.

- Laser scanning is often used to capture images of complex and hard-to-reach objects, such as buildings, bridges, and sculptures, that would be difficult to capture using traditional cameras.

2.1.2 Image to Coordinates

Image to Coordinates is the next step in photogrammetry after the object-to-image step. In this step, the information contained in the image is extracted and transformed into a set of coordinates that can be used to create a map or model of the physical world.

All this is done using specialized photogrammetry software that analyzes the image and identifies key features, such as points, lines, and surfaces, that can be used to establish the position and orientation of the image in space. The software then uses these features to calculate the coordinates of the image, taking into account factors such as the camera's position and orientation, the lens distortion, and the parameters of the imaging system.

The coordinates generated in this step are essential for creating accurate and reliable maps and models of the physical world. These coordinates can be used to create 2D maps, 3D models, or even virtual and augmented reality environments that provide an immersive experience of the physical world.

Examples

One example of the application of photogrammetry is in the field of archaeology, where photogrammetry is used to create 3D models of ancient ruins and artifacts. These models provide a detailed representation of the physical world and can be used to study and preserve the artifacts for future generations.

Another example is in the field of architecture, where photogrammetry is used to create precise and accurate models of buildings and structures. These models can be used to design renovations, conduct structural analysis, and simulate construction processes.

2.1.3 Coordinates to Map or Model

The final step in photogrammetry is to use the extracted coordinates to create a map or model of the physical world. This step involves transforming the coordinates into a common reference system, such as a geographic or cartesian coordinate system, and using them to create a representation of the world in two or three dimensions.

- In the case of two-dimensional maps, the coordinates are used to create a topographic map that displays the terrain and other features of the physical world. These maps are used for a wide range of applications, including navigation, land-use planning, and environmental management.

- In the case of three-dimensional models, the coordinates are used to create a detailed and accurate representation of the physical world. These models can be used for a variety of purposes, such as architectural design, urban planning, and virtual and augmented reality experiences.

One of the key benefits of photogrammetry is that it can produce highly accurate maps and models of the physical world. This is due to the high precision of the cameras and imaging systems used in photogrammetry, as well as the advanced software algorithms that are used to process and analyze the images.

Another benefit of photogrammetry is that it allows us to create maps and models of the physical world in real-time. This is particularly important in fields such as disaster response, where quick and accurate mapping of affected areas is critical for effective response and recovery efforts.

2.2 The Benefits of Photogrammetry over traditional ways

Photogrammetry has many benefits over traditional surveying and mapping methods.

2.2.1 Speed

The benefits of photogrammetry are numerous, and one of the key advantages is speed. Photogrammetry can be faster than traditional surveying and mapping methods, especially when used with unmanned aerial vehicles (UAVs), or drones. Drones equipped with high-resolution cameras and photogrammetry software can quickly capture images of large areas and process them into maps or models. This makes photogrammetry an efficient and cost-effective way to gather data for a wide range of applications, such as surveying land, monitoring crops, and inspecting infrastructure. Another benefit of photogrammetry is that it allows for frequent and repeated mapping.

For example, UAVs equipped with cameras can fly over an area multiple times to gather data and create updated maps or models. This makes it possible to monitor changes in an area over time, and to identify areas that require further attention or analysis.

In addition to speed, photogrammetry also offers several other benefits. It is a non-contact method of mapping, which means that it can be used in dangerous or difficult-to-access areas, such as in disaster zones, or on steep terrain.

2.2.2 Flexibility

Another important benefit of photogrammetry is its flexibility. Photogrammetry can be used to create maps and models of a wide range of scales, from large landscapes to small objects. This makes it possible to gather data for a variety of applications, such as urban planning, disaster response, and cultural heritage preservation.

For example, in urban planning, photogrammetry can be used to create detailed maps and models of cities, which can be used to analyze population density, transportation networks, and land use patterns. This information can be used to support decision-making around issues such as zoning, infrastructure development, and land use planning.

2.2.3 Quickly Assess

In disaster response, photogrammetry can be used to quickly assess the extent of damage and to monitor recovery efforts.

For example, UAVs equipped with cameras can fly over a disaster zone to gather high-resolution images, which can then be used to create maps and models of the area. This information can be used to identify areas that require immediate attention and to plan the deployment of resources.

In cultural heritage preservation, photogrammetry can be used to create detailed maps and models of historic sites, monuments, and buildings. This information can be used to document the condition of these sites and to support conservation and restoration efforts.

In addition to its applications in urban planning, disaster response, and cultural heritage preservation, photogrammetry is also used in a wide range of other industries, such as agriculture, forestry, mining, and construction.

2.2.4 Accuracy

Photogrammetry can be highly accurate, especially when multiple images are used to create a map or model. The accuracy of photogrammetry is dependent on the quality of the images, the software used to process them, and the quality control procedures used to validate the results. Modern photogrammetry software can automate many of the processes involved in mapping, reducing the risk of human error and increasing the accuracy of the final product.

In addition, the use of aerial imagery and UAVs allows for the collection of high-resolution data that can be used to create highly accurate maps and models. The use of ground control points, which are well-defined points on the ground used to verify the accuracy of the final product, can further improve the accuracy of photogrammetry. Photogrammetry can be used to support a wide range of applications, including surveying and mapping, engineering, and construction projects, where high accuracy is critical.

2.2.5 Cost-effectiveness

UAVs can significantly reduce the time and cost associated with collecting data, as they can cover large areas in a short period of time. The use of UAVs also eliminates the need for expensive equipment and personnel, as they can be operated by a single person. Furthermore, the cost of UAVs has significantly decreased in recent years, making them more accessible and affordable for a wider range of users.

In addition, the automation of many photogrammetry processes has reduced the need for manual labor, further reducing costs. Photogrammetry can also be used to collect data in difficult-to-reach or hazardous locations, reducing the need for additional safety measures and equipment.

The cost-effectiveness of photogrammetry makes it an attractive option for a wide range of applications, including environmental monitoring, urban planning, and infrastructure management.

2.3 Summary of the chapter

Photogrammetry is a powerful tool for measuring and understanding the physical world. Its benefits, combined with its growing accessibility and user-friendliness, make it an increasingly important tool for a wide range of applications, from disaster management and environmental monitoring to urban planning and cultural heritage preservation.

Chapter 3: Types of Photogrammetry

Photogrammetry can be divided into two main categories: aerial photogrammetry and close-range photogrammetry.

3.1 Aerial Photogrammetry

Aerial photogrammetry provides several advantages over traditional ground-based surveying and mapping methods, as it allows for the collection of data from a bird's-eye view. This perspective provides a unique and comprehensive view of the terrain, allowing for the detection of features and patterns that may not be visible from the ground. Furthermore, aerial photogrammetry can be used to create highly accurate maps and models, as the images can be taken from different angles and perspectives.

The use of UAVs in aerial photogrammetry has revolutionized the field in recent years, making it possible to collect data more efficiently and cost-effectively. UAVs are equipped with high-resolution cameras and GPS sensors, allowing them to gather detailed images of the terrain. In addition, UAVs can be operated in remote or difficult-to-reach locations, making it possible to gather data in areas that were previously inaccessible.

Aerial photogrammetry is widely used in a variety of applications, including urban planning, environmental monitoring, disaster response, and cultural heritage preservation. For example, aerial photogrammetry can be used to create detailed maps of urban areas, providing valuable information for urban planners and designers. It can also be used to monitor the health of forests and ecosystems, helping to identify areas that are in need of conservation or management. In addition, aerial photogrammetry can be used in disaster response efforts to quickly assess the extent of damage and identify areas that are in need of aid.

3.2 Close-Range Photogrammetry

Close-range photogrammetry is also known for its high precision, as the cameras used in this method are usually positioned very close to the object being captured, resulting in more detail in the final image. This level of detail is essential for many applications, such as architectural surveying, artifact documentation, and heritage preservation, where the accuracy of measurements is critical.

In close-range photogrammetry, the cameras used can either be film cameras or digital cameras. With the advent of digital cameras, close-range photogrammetry has become more accessible and affordable, allowing more people to use this method for various applications.

In addition, close-range photogrammetry can also be used in combination with other technologies, such as 3D laser scanning or structured light scanning, to create highly detailed maps and models. This hybrid approach can provide even greater accuracy and flexibility, making it a valuable tool for many different industries and disciplines.

Chapter 4: Applications of Photogrammetry

Photogrammetry is used in a wide variety of fields, including Surveying and Mapping, Architecture and Engineering, Environmental Science, Cultural Heritage and Archaeology, Disaster Management and Emergency Response.

4.1 Surveying and Mapping

Photogrammetry has a wide range of applications, including surveying and mapping. Surveying and mapping are critical for a variety of industries, including construction, civil engineering, urban planning, and natural resource management.

For example, in construction, photogrammetry is used to survey building sites and create accurate maps and models of existing structures. This information is used to plan and execute construction projects, as well as monitor progress and ensure that all work is being carried out according to specifications.

In urban planning, photogrammetry is used to create maps and models of cities and other populated areas. This information is used to plan and design new developments, as well as monitor and manage existing ones. For example, photogrammetry can be used to create a 3D model of a city, showing the location of roads, buildings, and other structures, as well as the location of parks, green spaces, and other amenities.

In natural resource management, photogrammetry is used to create maps and models of large areas of land, such as forests, wetlands, and other ecosystems. This information is used to plan and manage the use of natural resources, as well as monitor changes in the environment and assess the impact of human activities.

Photogrammetry is also used in cultural heritage preservation, where it is used to create maps and models of historic sites, monuments, and other cultural artifacts. This information is used to preserve and protect these important cultural treasures, as well as to study and understand their history and significance.

4.2 Architecture and Engineering

In the field of architecture and engineering, photogrammetry is a valuable tool for creating accurate and detailed models of buildings and structures. These models can be used for a variety of purposes, such as architectural design, structural analysis, and construction planning. For example, architects can use photogrammetry to create virtual walkthroughs of proposed building designs, allowing them to visualize and test different design options before construction begins. Engineers can use photogrammetry to create models of existing structures, which can then be used to perform detailed structural analysis and determine the best approach for renovation or reinforcement.

In construction, photogrammetry can be used to monitor progress on a building site and ensure that everything is being built according to plan.

By taking regular photographs of the construction site and using photogrammetry to create a detailed map or model, engineers and contractors can easily compare the current state of the construction to the plans and quickly identify any deviations or problems. This helps to ensure that the final product meets all specifications and requirements, and reduces the risk of costly mistakes or delays.

4.3 Environmental Science

Photogrammetry has proven to be a valuable tool for environmental scientists in monitoring and studying the environment. It can be used to assess the impact of natural disasters and human activities on ecosystems, such as forests, wetlands, and bodies of water. Photogrammetry can also be used to track changes in the landscape over time, which can help scientists to better understand the impact of climate change, habitat loss, and other environmental issues.

For example, researchers can use aerial photogrammetry to map the extent and distribution of forests, wetlands, and other ecosystems. By analyzing images captured by UAVs or satellites, they can accurately measure the size, shape, and distribution of different ecosystems, as well as changes in their extent over time. This information can be used to track the health and productivity of ecosystems, as well as to develop conservation and management plans.

In addition, photogrammetry can be used to monitor the progress of restoration and reforestation projects. By capturing images of the same area over time, researchers can track the growth of new plantings and assess their success in establishing new ecosystems. This information is critical for ensuring the long-term success of restoration projects, and for understanding the role that restoration can play in mitigating the impacts of environmental degradation.

4.4 Cultural Heritage and Archaeology

In cultural heritage and archaeology, photogrammetry plays an important role in the documentation and preservation of cultural heritage sites, such as ancient ruins, historic buildings, and monuments. This technology allows researchers to create accurate, detailed 3D models of these sites, which can be used to study and understand their cultural and historical context. For example, photogrammetry can be used to document the intricate details of ancient temple structures, to create a record of their appearance before they undergo preservation or restoration work.

In addition, photogrammetry can be used to monitor the changes that occur over time in cultural heritage sites, such as the gradual erosion of stone structures or the growth of vegetation around ruins. This information can be used to develop preservation and restoration plans, as well as to track the progress of conservation work.

Furthermore, photogrammetry can also be used in the field of archaeology to create detailed maps of excavation sites, which can be used to study the spatial relationships between artifacts and other elements, such as structures and features. This information is crucial in reconstructing and understanding the context of ancient civilizations, and can provide insights into the organization and use of space in the past. Additionally, photogrammetry can be used to preserve the memory of endangered or threatened cultural heritage sites, by creating 3D models that can be used for research and education purposes, even if the physical sites are no longer accessible. For example, photogrammetry was used to create a detailed 3D model of the ancient city of Palmyra in Syria, which was partially destroyed by conflict in 2015. The model allowed researchers to continue their studies of the city's architecture and history, even as the physical site was being damaged.

4.5 Disaster Management and Emergency Response

In the event of a natural disaster, photogrammetry can play a critical role in helping to manage the response and recovery efforts. By using aerial or close-range photogrammetry, it is possible to quickly gather detailed data about the extent of the damage and the affected areas. This information can then be used to inform decision-making, such as the allocation of resources and the prioritization of recovery efforts.

For example, after a hurricane, photogrammetry can be used to create detailed maps of the affected areas, highlighting areas that have been impacted by flooding, wind damage, and other hazards. This information can then be used by emergency responders and relief organizations to quickly and effectively deploy resources, such as food, water, and medical supplies, to those in need.

In addition, photogrammetry can also be used to monitor the recovery efforts over time, helping to ensure that progress is being made and that resources are being used effectively. This can be especially important in large-scale disasters, where it can be difficult to get a clear understanding of the overall situation.

Chapter 5: Equipment Used in Photogrammetry

Photogrammetry relies on a range of equipment, from cameras to software, to capture and process images and create maps, models, and other visual representations of the world.

5.1 Cameras

The most important piece of equipment in photogrammetry is the camera. Photogrammetry cameras come in many shapes and sizes, but they all have the same basic function: to take photographs.

Cameras used in photogrammetry can be divided into two main categories: aerial cameras and terrestrial cameras. Aerial cameras are typically used to capture images from the air, while terrestrial cameras are used to capture images from the ground.

5.1.1 Aerial cameras

Aerial cameras used in photogrammetry have come a long way over the years and now offer a range of advanced features and capabilities. Modern aerial cameras are designed to provide high-resolution images with minimal distortion and maximum accuracy. They typically use large-format sensors, which can capture more detail and information than smaller sensors, and high-resolution lenses, which can provide clear and sharp images from long distances.

Additionally, many modern aerial cameras are equipped with GPS and IMU sensors, which help to accurately determine the position and orientation of the camera at the time the images were captured. This information is critical for photogrammetry, as it is used to transform the images into a common reference system and to create maps and models of the physical world.

Aerial cameras are also designed to be easy to use, even in challenging environments. They are often equipped with features such as automatic exposure and focus control, as well as user-friendly software interfaces, to allow operators to quickly and efficiently capture the images they need. Some aerial cameras are even equipped with advanced features, such as automated flight planning and real-time image transmission, that make it possible to gather data quickly and efficiently, even in remote or difficult-to-reach locations.

A key benefit of aerial cameras is their ability to capture large amounts of high-resolution data in a relatively short amount of time. For example, a single flight with a UAV equipped with an aerial camera can gather data over an area of several square kilometers in just a few hours. This makes it possible to generate detailed maps and models of large areas in a relatively short amount of time, which is especially important in the case of disaster management and emergency response efforts.

Another important feature of aerial cameras is their ability to capture images at different times and under different lighting conditions. This makes it possible to generate accurate and up-to-date maps and models of large areas, even in the face of rapidly changing conditions. For example, aerial cameras can be used to generate maps of rapidly changing landscapes, such as coastal zones or areas affected by natural disasters, in real-time.

5.1.2 Terrestrial cameras

Terrestrial cameras used in photogrammetry typically have smaller sensors and lower resolution lenses compared to aerial cameras. However, they are designed to be compact and portable, making them ideal for use in close-range photogrammetry applications. These cameras are often equipped with features such as manual exposure control and interchangeable lenses, which give the user more control over the image capture process. Some terrestrial cameras also have built-in GPS and IMU sensors, which can be used to help improve the accuracy of the final map or model. They can also be mounted on tripods or other stabilizing devices to help ensure that images are captured accurately. Terrestrial cameras are commonly used in architectural and engineering applications, cultural heritage and archaeology, and for capturing images of objects for 3D printing and virtual reality applications.

They provide powerful and efficient tools for processing and analyzing images, such as automatic feature detection, 3D reconstruction, and georeferencing. They also allow users to create maps, models, and digital terrain models from the images, which can be used for a wide range of applications, such as surveying and mapping, architecture and engineering, environmental science, cultural heritage and archaeology, and disaster management and emergency response. Some software programs even provide advanced capabilities such as support for multi-camera systems, dense cloud generation, and texture mapping, which can enhance the accuracy and quality of the final output. With user-friendly interfaces and intuitive workflows, these software programs make photogrammetry accessible to a wide range of users, including professionals, hobbyists, and students.

5.2 Software

Photogrammetry software is used to process images and create maps, models, and other visual representations of the world. There are many different photogrammetry software programs available, each with its own unique features and capabilities.

Some of the most popular photogrammetry software programs include Agisoft Photoscan, Pix4D, and DroneDeploy. These programs are designed to work with a wide range of images and data, including aerial images captured by UAVs and terrestrial images captured by ground-based cameras. Disadvantage of these programs is they are expensive. Three alternatives, suitable for beginners and to be purchased with a somewhat lower budget are: 3DF Zephyr, Photoscanner and Autodesk ReCap Photo. Let's take a closer look at this software.

5.2.1 Agisoft Photoscan

Agisoft Photoscan is a powerful and widely used photogrammetry software program designed to convert photos into 3D models and maps. The program is designed to be highly flexible and works with a wide variety of images and data, including aerial images captured by unmanned aerial vehicles (UAVs) and terrestrial imagery captured by ground-based cameras. We will examine the main features and benefits of Agisoft Photoscan, as well as the pros and cons of the program, to help you better understand how it can be used in the field of photogrammetry.

Features:

Agisoft Photoscan is a highly advanced photogrammetry software program that is packed with features to help you create high-quality 3D models and maps.

Some of the main features of Agisoft Photosan are:

High-quality 3D modeling

Agisoft Photoscan uses advanced algorithms to create highly accurate and detailed 3D models from photographs. The program is designed to work with a wide range of image types and formats, including images captured by UAVs and terrestrial cameras.

Advanced image processing

Agisoft Photoscan is equipped with advanced image processing tools that help to ensure accurate and reliable results. The program is designed to handle images captured under a wide range of lighting and weather conditions, as well as images captured from different perspectives.

Powerful mapping tools

Agisoft Photoscan includes a wide range of mapping tools, making it easy to create accurate and detailed maps of large areas, such as cities, regions, or entire countries. The program can also be used to produce highly accurate and detailed maps of smaller areas, such as buildings and monuments.

User-friendly interface

Agisoft Photoscan is designed to be easy to use, even for users with limited photogrammetry experience. The program features a user-friendly interface that makes it easy to access and use the various tools and features included in the software.

Pros and Cons

While Agisoft Photoscan is a highly effective and widely-used photogrammetry software program, it is not without its pros and cons.

Pros:

High-quality results: Agisoft Photoscan is designed to produce highly accurate and detailed 3D models and maps, making it ideal for use in a wide range of applications.

- User-friendly interface: The program features a user-friendly interface that makes it easy to access and use the various tools and features available. This makes it accessible for users with varying levels of experience and technical knowledge.
- Supports a wide range of file formats: Agisoft Photoscan supports a wide range of file formats, including JPEG, TIFF, and RAW images, making it easy to work with images captured by different cameras and devices.
- Integration with other tools: Agisoft Photoscan integrates with other photogrammetry software and tools, such as GIS and CAD programs, making it possible to use the results of photogrammetry projects in a wider range of applications.
- Automated processes: Many of the processes in Agisoft Photoscan are automated, including image alignment and 3D model generation, making it faster and easier to produce high-quality results.

Cons:

- Higher learning curve: Although the user interface is user-friendly, the program is more complex than some other photogrammetry software options, which may require a higher learning curve for some users.

- Resource-intensive: Agisoft Photoscan is a resource-intensive program, which may require a more powerful computer to run effectively.
- Expensive: Compared to other photogrammetry software options, Agisoft Photoscan is relatively expensive, which may make it less accessible for some users.

5.2.2 Pix4D

Pix4D is a photogrammetry software program designed to convert images into highly accurate and detailed 3D models and maps. It is widely used in various industries such as construction, agriculture, mining, surveying, and environmental monitoring. We will discuss the features, modeling, image processing, tools, and interface of Pix4D.

Features

Pix4D offers a wide range of features that enable users to create highly detailed and accurate 3D models and maps. Some of its features include:

- Aerial and ground image processing: Pix4D can process both aerial and ground images to create 3D models and maps.
- Point cloud and mesh generation: The software can generate point clouds and meshes from images to create accurate 3D models.
  - Point cloud and mesh generation are techniques used in 3D modeling and mapping to create highly detailed and

accurate representations of real-world objects or environments.

- o A point cloud is a collection of 3D points that represent the surface of an object or environment. These points are usually captured using various sensors that create a 3D scan of the object or its surroundings.
- o Once a point cloud has been generated, it can be made into a mesh. A mesh is a collection of vertices, edges, and faces that make up a 3D object. Mesh generation connects the points in the point cloud to create a surface that accurately represents the object or environment being modeled.
- o The resulting 3D model or map can be used for a variety of applications, such as virtual reality, video games, architectural visualization, and engineering design. The level of detail and accuracy achieved in the model or map depends on the quality and density of the point cloud, as well as the algorithms used to generate the mesh.
- Multispectral processing: Pix4D can process multispectral images to create detailed maps of crop health and vegetation.
  - o Multispectral sensors capture images of an area using different wavelengths of light. The resulting images show what the area looks like in each wavelength, which can reveal information about plant health and vitality. For example, healthy vegetation reflects more near-infrared light and less green light than unhealthy vegetation.

- Using multispectral processing, Pix4D can combine the information from the different bands of light to make a more comprehensive analysis of vegetation health and vigor. The software can generate maps that highlight areas of the crop that are healthy, stressed or diseased. These maps can be used by farmers to identify areas that need more attention or treatment.
- Orthomosaic creation: The software can create high-resolution orthomosaic maps that are georeferenced and accurately aligned.
  - When creating an orthomosaic map, multiple overlapping aerial or satellite images of an area are stitched together to create a single, high-resolution, georeferenced image.
  - When creating an orthomosaic, Pix4D uses photogrammetry algorithms to align the images and remove distortions caused by differences in the angle and height of the images. This results in a seamless and accurate representation of the area being mapped.
  - In addition to creating a visually appealing map, Pix4D also ensures that the orthomosaic is georeferenced, meaning it can be positioned accurately in real-world coordinates. This allows the map to be used for precise measurements and analysis, such as determining distances, areas, and volumes of objects on the map.
- Automatic and manual tie point generation: Pix4D can automatically generate tie points between images, or users can manually add tie points to improve the accuracy of the model.

- Volume and area calculation: The software can calculate the volume and area of objects in the 3D model.
- Inspection tools: Pix4D offers inspection tools to identify and measure objects in the 3D model.

Modeling

Pix4D takes images and uses algorithms to calculate the position and orientation of each image in 3D space. The software then creates a point cloud and mesh from the images, which are used to create the 3D model.

Image Processing

The image processing in Pix4D is divided into three stages: Initial processing, point cloud and mesh generation, and DSM and orthomosaic generation.

- Initial processing: In this stage, the software analyzes the images and extracts key features such as tie points and camera positions.
- Point cloud and mesh generation: In this stage, the software creates a 3D point cloud and mesh from the images.
- DSM and orthomosaic generation: In this stage, the software generates a digital surface model (DSM) and orthomosaic from the point cloud and mesh.
    - A digital surface model (DSM) is a 3D representation of a surface or terrain created using data collected through photogrammetry.

Tools

Pix4D offers a range of tools to help users create accurate 3D models and maps. Some of its tools include:

- Calibration: Pix4D allows users to calibrate their cameras to improve the accuracy of the model.
- GCPs: The software allows users to add ground control points (GCPs) to improve the accuracy of the model.
- Point cloud editing: Pix4D offers a point cloud editing tool to help users clean up their point clouds and remove noise.
- Annotations: The software allows users to annotate their models to identify and measure objects.

Interface

Pix4D has a user-friendly interface that is easy to navigate. The software has a project-based approach, where users can create new projects, load existing projects, or open recent projects. The interface is divided into several sections, including the 3D model view, image view, and project settings. The 3D model view allows users to view and manipulate their 3D models, while the image view allows users to view their images and add tie points. The project settings section allows users to configure various settings such as processing options, camera calibration, and GCPs.

Pros:

- High accuracy: Pix4D is known for producing highly accurate results, making it a popular choice for many professionals in the field. This accuracy is achieved through the use of advanced algorithms and features that enable the program to extract precise information from images.
- Compatibility: Pix4D is compatible with a wide range of image sources, including aerial images captured by UAVs and terrestrial images captured by ground-based cameras. This makes it a flexible and versatile tool for use in many different applications.
- Ease of use: Pix4D features a user-friendly interface that makes it easy to access and use the various tools and features. This makes it a good choice for professionals who are new to photogrammetry or who need to complete projects quickly and efficiently.

Cons:

- Cost: Pix4D can be expensive compared to some other photogrammetry software programs, which may be a barrier for some users.
- Complexity: While Pix4D is designed to be user-friendly, some of the more advanced features can be complex and difficult to use. This may make it a less appealing option for some professionals who are looking for a simpler solution.
- Memory requirements: Pix4D can be demanding in terms of system resources, and may require a high-end computer to run

effectively. This may be a barrier for some users who do not have access to a powerful machine.

5.2.3 DroneDeploy

DroneDeploy is a popular photogrammetry software program designed to convert images into highly accurate and detailed 3D models and maps. It is widely used in various industries such as agriculture, construction, mining, surveying, and environmental monitoring. Let's dive a bit deeper into DroneDeploy.

Features:

DroneDeploy offers a range of features that allow users to create highly detailed and accurate 3D models and maps. Some of its features include:

- Aerial and ground image processing: The software can process both aerial and ground images to create 3D models and maps.

- Point cloud and mesh generation: DroneDeploy can generate point clouds and meshes from images to create accurate 3D models.

- Volume and area calculation: The software can calculate the volume and area of objects in the 3D model.

- Multispectral processing: DroneDeploy can process multispectral images to create detailed maps of crop health and vegetation.

- Orthomosaic creation: The software can create high-resolution orthomosaic maps that are georeferenced and accurately aligned.

- Automatic and manual tie point generation: DroneDeploy can automatically generate tie points between images, or users can manually add tie points to improve the accuracy of the model.

- 3D modeling of structures: DroneDeploy can create 3D models of structures such as buildings and bridges.

Modeling:

DroneDeploy uses photogrammetry to create 3D models and maps. The software takes images and uses algorithms to calculate the position and orientation of each image in 3D space. The software then creates a point cloud and mesh from the images, which are used to create the 3D model.

Image Processing: The image processing in DroneDeploy is divided into four stages: Uploading, processing, inspecting, and sharing.

- Uploading: In this stage, users upload their images to the software.

- Processing: In this stage, the software analyzes the images and extracts key features such as tie points and camera positions.

- Inspecting: In this stage, users can inspect their 3D models and maps, add annotations, and perform measurements.

- Sharing: In this stage, users can share their 3D models and maps with others.

Tools:

DroneDeploy offers a range of tools to help users create accurate 3D models and maps. Some of its tools include:

- Annotations: The software allows users to annotate their models to identify and measure objects.

- Elevation profile: DroneDeploy offers an elevation profile tool to help users analyze the terrain.

- GCPs: The software allows users to add ground control points (GCPs) to improve the accuracy of the model.

- 3D structures: DroneDeploy can create 3D models of structures such as buildings and bridges.

Interface:

DroneDeploy has a user-friendly interface that is easy to navigate. The software has a project-based approach, where users can create new projects, load existing projects, or open recent projects. The interface is divided into several sections, including the 3D model view, image view, and project settings. The 3D model view allows users to view and manipulate their 3D models, while the image view allows users to view their images and add tie points. The project settings section allows users to configure various settings such as processing options, camera calibration, and GCPs.

- Easy to Use: DroneDeploy has a user-friendly interface that makes it easy for users to access and use the various tools and features of the program, even if they have limited experience with photogrammetry.
- Automatic Processing: DroneDeploy has a powerful automatic processing feature that allows users to quickly and easily process large amounts of image data, even in challenging environments. The program automatically detects and processes images, reducing the amount of manual work required.
- High-quality Results: DroneDeploy is designed to produce highly accurate and detailed 3D models and maps, making it ideal for use in a wide range of applications. The program uses advanced algorithms and machine learning techniques to produce the best possible results, even in complex environments.
- Integration with Drones: DroneDeploy is designed specifically for use with UAVs, and is fully integrated with the most popular drone platforms. This makes it easy for users to access and use the program in the field, and allows for seamless data transfer between the drone and the software.

Cons:

- Expensive: DroneDeploy can be a more expensive option than other photogrammetry software programs, especially for users who require advanced features or are working with large amounts of data.

- Limited Platform Support: DroneDeploy is designed specifically for use with UAVs, and may not be suitable for users who require support for other data sources, such as ground-based cameras or satellite imagery.
- Complex Processing: DroneDeploy's automatic processing features can make it a complex program to use, especially for users who are new to photogrammetry. This can be a challenge for users who require detailed control over the processing and analysis of their data.
- Despite these limitations, DroneDeploy is widely regarded as one of the most powerful and effective photogrammetry software programs available. Its integration with UAVs, easy-to-use interface, and automatic processing features make it ideal for a wide range of applications, including surveying and mapping, environmental science, and disaster management.

5.2.4 3DF Zephyr

3DF Zephyr is a photogrammetry software program designed to convert images into highly accurate and detailed 3D models and maps. It is widely used in various industries such as architecture, engineering, construction, and cultural heritage. We will discuss the features, modeling, image processing, tools, and interface of 3DF Zephyr.

Features:

3DF Zephyr offers a range of features that allow users to create highly detailed and accurate 3D models and maps. Some of its features include:

- Aerial and ground image processing: The software can process both aerial and ground images to create 3D models and maps.

- Point cloud and mesh generation: 3DF Zephyr can generate point clouds and meshes from images to create accurate 3D models.

- Volume and area calculation: The software can calculate the volume and area of objects in the 3D model.

- Texture mapping: 3DF Zephyr can create high-quality texture maps for 3D models.

- Orthophoto generation: The software can create orthophoto maps that are georeferenced and accurately aligned.

    - An orthophoto is a type of aerial photograph that has been geometrically corrected so that it can be used as a map. Orthophotos are usually created by taking aerial images with a camera mounted on an aircraft or drone and then processing the images using specialized software.

- Automatic and manual tie point generation: 3DF Zephyr can automatically generate tie points between images, or users can manually add tie points to improve the accuracy of the model.

- Dense reconstruction: The software can perform dense reconstruction to create highly detailed 3D models.

Modeling:

3DF Zephyr uses photogrammetry to create 3D models and maps. The software takes images and uses algorithms to calculate the position and orientation of each image in 3D space. The software then creates a point cloud and mesh from the images, which are used to create the 3D model.

Image Processing:

The image processing in 3DF Zephyr is divided into three stages: Calibration, reconstruction, and post-processing.

- Calibration: In this stage, users can calibrate their cameras to improve the accuracy of the model.

- Reconstruction: In this stage, the software analyzes the images and extracts key features such as tie points and camera positions.

- Post-processing: In this stage, users can refine their 3D models, add texture maps, and perform measurements.

Tools:

3DF Zephyr offers a range of tools to help users create accurate 3D models and maps. Some of its tools include:

- Annotations: The software allows users to annotate their models to identify and measure objects.

- Volume and area calculation: 3DF Zephyr can calculate the volume and area of objects in the 3D model.

- Texture mapping: The software can create high-quality texture maps for 3D models.

- Georeferencing: 3DF Zephyr can georeference 3D models to align them with real-world

Pros:

One of the key features of 3DF Zephyr is its ability to process large volumes of images, which makes it ideal for use in large-scale mapping and surveying projects. The program can also work with a wide range of images, including aerial images captured by UAVs and terrestrial images captured by ground-based cameras.

Another advantage of 3DF Zephyr is its user-friendly interface, which makes it easy for beginners to access and use the various tools and features. The program also comes with a comprehensive set of tutorials and online resources, making it easy to get started and quickly become proficient in using the software.

Cons:

In terms of cons, 3DF Zephyr may not be as feature-rich as some of the more expensive photogrammetry software programs on the market. However, for many users, this is outweighed by the program's affordability and ease of use.

Additionally, some users may find that the software is less flexible than other photogrammetry programs in terms of the types of images and data that can be processed.

5.2.5 Photoscanner

Photoscanner is a photogrammetry software program that enables users to create 3D models and maps from photos. It is developed by Agisoft LLC, a company based in St. Petersburg, Russia. Photoscanner is a powerful tool that can be used in a variety of industries, including architecture, engineering, construction, archaeology, and surveying. In this chapter, we will explore the various features, modeling, image processing, tools and interface of Photoscanner.

Features:

Photoscanner offers a range of features that make it a versatile and powerful tool for photogrammetry. Some of its notable features are:

- Multi-view Stereo Reconstruction: Photoscanner uses a multi-view stereo reconstruction algorithm that combines information from multiple photos to create a 3D model. This algorithm is highly accurate and can create detailed models of objects and environments.

- Dense Point Cloud and Mesh Generation: Photoscanner generates a dense point cloud from the input photos, which is then used to create a 3D mesh. The mesh can be used for visualization, analysis, and further processing.

- A dense point cloud is a collection of 3D points that represent the surface of an object or terrain. Dense point clouds are usually generated using photogrammetry, which can capture a large number of data points with high accuracy and resolution.

  - To turn a dense point cloud into a 3D mesh, specialized software is used that uses algorithms to convert the individual data points into a connected network of triangles ("meshing"). The result is a 3D model that approximates the shape of the original object or terrain.

- Image Alignment and Calibration: Photoscanner automatically aligns and calibrates the input photos to ensure that they are accurately placed in the 3D model. This helps to minimize errors and inaccuracies in the final model.

- Texture Mapping: Photoscanner can generate texture maps for the 3D model by projecting the input photos onto the surface of the mesh. This creates a highly realistic and detailed model that can be used for visualization and analysis.

- Orthophoto Generation: Photoscanner can generate orthophotos, which are 2D maps that are georeferenced and corrected for distortion. Orthophotos can be used for mapping, surveying, and other applications.

Modeling:

Modeling with Photoscanner Photoscanner offers a range of modeling options that allow users to create detailed and accurate 3D models.

- Sparse Point Cloud Generation: Photoscanner can generate a sparse point cloud, which is a collection of points that represent the position of the input photos. The sparse point cloud can be used to create a rough 3D model, which can then be refined using other modeling tools.

- Polygon Editing: Photoscanner allows users to edit the 3D mesh by adding or removing polygons. This can be useful for creating complex models or for removing unwanted features from the model.

- Texture Editing: Photoscanner allows users to edit the texture map by adjusting the brightness, contrast, and color of the input photos. This can be useful for enhancing the visual quality of the model.

- Measurement Tools: Photoscanner provides a range of measurement tools that allow users to measure distances, areas, and volumes in the 3D model. This can be useful for analysis and planning.

Image Processing:

Photoscanner offers a range of image processing tools that allow users to optimize the input photos for photogrammetry. Some of the image processing features are:

- Image Filtering: Photoscanner can filter the input photos to remove noise and improve their quality. This can be useful for improving the accuracy of the 3D model.

- Depth Map Generation: Photoscanner can generate a depth map from the input photos, which is used to create the 3D model. The depth map can be used to adjust the focus and depth of field of the input photos.

- HDR Imaging: Photoscanner supports HDR imaging, which allows users to capture a wide range of lighting conditions in the input photos. This can be useful for creating highly detailed and realistic models.

- Color Correction: Photoscanner can correct the color of the input photos to ensure that they are consistent across the entire model. This is particularly important when working with images taken under different lighting conditions or from different cameras. Color correction helps to ensure that the final 3D model has accurate colors that reflect the real-world object or environment.

Photoscanner offers a range of color correction tools, including automatic and manual options. The automatic color correction tool analyzes the input photos and adjusts their colors to ensure consistency. This is useful for quickly correcting color inconsistencies in large sets of photos.

For more precise color correction, Photoscanner offers a manual color correction tool that allows users to adjust the color balance, saturation, and brightness of individual photos. This can be useful for fine-tuning the colors of the 3D model to match the real-world object or environment.

In addition to color correction, Photoscanner also offers tools for adjusting exposure, contrast, and sharpness. These tools can be used to improve the overall quality of the input photos and ensure that the 3D model has accurate and detailed textures.

Interface and Tools

Photoscanner has a user-friendly interface that allows users to easily import, process, and model their photos. The interface is divided into several panels, including the workspace, photo browser, and processing pane.

The workspace is where the 3D model is displayed, and users can interact with it using the various modeling tools. The photo browser allows users to view and select the input photos, and the processing pane displays the progress of the photogrammetry process.

Photoscanner offers a range of modeling tools, including selection tools, brush tools, and transform tools. These tools allow users to select and manipulate individual polygons, vertices, and edges, and adjust the position, rotation, and scale of the model.

Photoscanner also offers a range of analysis tools, including measurement tools, volume calculation tools, and contour generation tools. These tools allow users to analyze and measure the 3D model and extract valuable information for further processing and analysis.

Pros:

- Ease of Use: Photoscanner is known for its ease of use, making it ideal for beginners who are just starting to learn about photogrammetry. The user interface is intuitive and straightforward, allowing users to quickly get started and start producing results.
- Affordable: Compared to some of the more expensive photogrammetry software programs, Photoscanner is relatively affordable. This makes it an ideal option for those who are just starting out or who are working with limited budgets.
- Compatibility: Photoscanner is compatible with a wide range of photos, including those taken with drones, cameras, and smartphones. This allows users to work with the photos they have available and to create 3D models and maps from these photos with ease.

Cons:

- Limited Features: Photoscanner is designed for beginners, and as a result, it may not have all of the features that more advanced users need. This can be a drawback for those who need to create more complex models or who require additional features.

- Quality of Results: While Photoscanner is designed to produce high-quality results, it may not produce the same level of detail and accuracy as some of the more expensive photogrammetry software programs. This can be a drawback for those who need the highest level of accuracy possible.

5.2.6 Autodesk ReCap Photo

Autodesk ReCap Photo is a photogrammetry software program designed to work with photos and other images to create highly accurate 3D models and maps. This software is developed by Autodesk, which is a leading company in providing software solutions for architecture, engineering, construction, and manufacturing industries. ReCap Photo is an essential tool for professionals who require accurate 3D models and maps for their projects, such as architects, surveyors, and engineers. Let's take a closer look at Autodesk ReCap Photo.

Features:

Autodesk ReCap Photo offers a wide range of features that make it a comprehensive photogrammetry software. Some of the key features of ReCap Photo are:

- High-Resolution Processing: ReCap Photo can process images with a high resolution of up to 100 megapixels, enabling the creation of highly detailed 3D models and maps.

- 3D Modeling: ReCap Photo provides a suite of tools for creating 3D models from photos and other images. These tools include mesh creation, texture mapping, and point cloud editing.

- Aerial Mapping: ReCap Photo can be used for aerial mapping, which is the process of creating 3D maps from aerial photographs. This feature is particularly useful for surveyors and engineers who require accurate maps for their projects.

- Point Cloud Processing: ReCap Photo can process point cloud data, which is a collection of 3D points that represent the surface of an object. This feature is useful for creating accurate 3D models of complex objects.

- Customizable Outputs: ReCap Photo allows users to customize the output of their 3D models and maps by adjusting parameters such as resolution, texture quality, and color balance.

Modeling:

ReCap Photo offers several tools for creating 3D models from photos and other images. The modeling process typically involves the following steps:

- Image Import: The first step in creating a 3D model is to import the photos or images into ReCap Photo.

- Image Alignment: ReCap Photo uses advanced algorithms to align the images and determine their position and orientation in 3D space.

- Point Cloud Generation: ReCap Photo generates a point cloud from the aligned images, which represents the surface of the object being modeled.

- Mesh Creation: ReCap Photo creates a mesh from the point cloud, which is a collection of polygons that represent the surface of the object.

- Texture Mapping: ReCap Photo applies textures to the mesh, which gives it a realistic appearance.

Image Processing:

ReCap Photo uses advanced algorithms to process images and generate accurate 3D models and maps. Some of the key image processing features of ReCap Photo are:

- Image Alignment: ReCap Photo uses feature matching algorithms to align images and determine their position and orientation in 3D space.

- Feature Extraction: ReCap Photo extracts features from images, such as corners and edges, which are used to align the images and generate a point cloud.

- Stereo Reconstruction: ReCap Photo uses stereo reconstruction algorithms to calculate the depth of objects in images, which is used to generate a point cloud.

- Color Balancing: ReCap Photo applies color balancing algorithms to images, which adjusts the color and brightness of the images to create a uniform appearance.

Tools:

- Camera Calibration: The camera calibration tool is used to optimize the camera settings for capturing images. It helps to ensure that the captured images are aligned correctly and result in a highly accurate 3D model. Users can adjust camera settings such as lens distortion, focal length, and image format.

- Point Cloud Editing: ReCap Photo allows users to edit point clouds by adding, removing, or adjusting individual points. This is an important step in the 3D modeling process and can greatly improve the accuracy and quality of 3D models.

- Texture: Texture is an essential component of 3D modeling and is used to create the appearance of surface characteristics on a 3D model. In ReCap Photo, textures can be applied to 3D models using images or photos. This helps to create realistic and visually appealing 3D models.

- Meshing: The meshing tool is used to create a 3D mesh from the point cloud. The mesh can be further edited to create a highly detailed 3D model.

- Export: Once the 3D model is complete, users can export it in a variety of file formats such as OBJ, FBX, and STL.

Interface:

The user interface of ReCap Photo is designed to be user-friendly and intuitive. Here are some of the key features of the interface:

- Navigation Panel: The navigation panel provides access to various tools and settings such as camera calibration, point cloud editing, and meshing.

- Viewer: The viewer displays the 3D model and allows users to zoom in and out, rotate, and pan the model.

- Toolbar: The toolbar provides quick access to commonly used tools such as the camera calibration tool, point cloud editing tool, and texture tool.

- Status Bar: The status bar displays important information about the current project, such as the number of images processed and the accuracy of the point cloud.

- Project Panel: The project panel displays a list of all the projects created in ReCap Photo. Users can easily switch between projects and access their settings.

Pros:

- High-quality results: Autodesk ReCap Photo is designed to produce highly accurate and detailed 3D models and maps, making it ideal for use in a wide range of applications.

- Easy to use: The program features a user-friendly interface that makes it easy to access and use the various tools and features.

- Integration with other software: Autodesk ReCap Photo can be integrated with other Autodesk software, such as AutoCAD and Revit, to provide a seamless workflow for users.

- Wide range of applications: The program can be used in a wide range of applications, including surveying and mapping, architecture and engineering, environmental science, and cultural heritage and archaeology.

Cons:

- Cost: Autodesk ReCap Photo is a premium software program, and its cost may be a barrier for some users, especially beginners or those on a tight budget.

- Complexity: While the program is designed to be easy to use, it may still be complex for some users, especially beginners, and may require some training to master.

5.3 Other Equipment

In addition to cameras and software, photogrammetry relies on a range of other equipment to ensure the accuracy and reliability of the images captured. GPS and IMU (Inertial Measurement Unit) sensors are two of the most important pieces of equipment used in photogrammetry.

GPS sensors provide information about the location of the camera at the time of image capture. This information is used to georeference the images, allowing them to be accurately positioned on a map. GPS data can be used to create maps and models that are highly accurate, making it an essential component of many photogrammetry applications, such as surveying and mapping, environmental science, and disaster management and emergency response.

IMU sensors, on the other hand, capture data about the orientation and motion of the camera during image capture. This data is used to correct for any lens distortion or image warping that may occur during image capture. IMU sensors can also be used to help ensure that images are aligned correctly with one another, which is essential for producing accurate 3D models and maps.

Control points and ground control points are also important pieces of equipment in photogrammetry. Control points are physical markers that are placed at known locations within the scene being captured. These markers are used to provide a reference for the photogrammetry software, helping to ensure that the images are aligned correctly with one another. Ground control points, on the other hand, are markers that are placed at known locations on the ground. These markers are used to help ensure that the images are accurately positioned on a map.

Control points and ground control points are used to help ensure accurate and reliable maps and models. Control points are markers placed on the ground that help to align images and ensure that the maps and models are accurate. Ground control points are markers placed on the ground that are used to validate and refine maps and models.

Photogrammetry relies on a range of equipment, including cameras, software, GPS and IMU sensors, control points, and ground control points. Each piece of equipment plays an important role in capturing and processing images and creating accurate and reliable maps and models of the world. The increasing accessibility and affordability of photogrammetry equipment, including UAVs and photogrammetry software, has made it easier and more accessible than ever before.

Chapter 7: The Basics of Drone Photogrammetry

Drone photogrammetry involves using a drone to capture images of a particular area, and then using photogrammetry software to turn those images into a map or a 3D model. This allows for the measurement of distances and angles between objects in the images, which can then be used to create a detailed map or model. Drone photogrammetry can be used for a variety of purposes, including surveying, mapping, and inspection.

7.1 Types of Drone Photogrammetry Techniques

There are several techniques that are commonly used in drone photogrammetry. These include:

- Overlapping Image Method: This method involves capturing images of an area from multiple angles so that the images overlap. The photogrammetry software then uses these overlapping images to create a 3D model.

- Structure from Motion (SfM): This method involves capturing images of an object or area while the drone is in motion. The photogrammetry software uses the motion of the drone to create a 3D model.

- Multi-View Stereo (MVS): This method involves capturing images of an area from multiple angles, and then using photogrammetry software to create a 3D model. This method can be used to create highly detailed models with a high level of accuracy.

- Remote Sensing: This method involves using drones equipped with specialized sensors, analyzed to gain valuable insights about the environment and make informed decisions about how best to manage and utilize it.

Remote sensing using drones is a rapidly growing field, with a wide range of applications in industries such as agriculture, forestry, and natural resource management. In agriculture, for example, drone-based remote sensing can be used to gather data about crop health and growth patterns, allowing farmers to make informed decisions about when to water, fertilize, and harvest their crops.

In forestry, drone-based remote sensing can be used to monitor and manage forest health, detect areas of damage, and track changes in the forest over time. This information can be used to make informed decisions about the management and conservation of the forest, as well as to detect and respond to threats such as wildfires and insect infestations.

In natural resource management, drone-based remote sensing can be used to monitor and manage wildlife populations, track changes in ecosystems, and gather data about the health of wetlands and other sensitive habitats. This information can be used to make informed decisions about the conservation and management of these habitats, as well as to detect and respond to threats such as pollution and habitat loss.

The use of drones for remote sensing is a powerful tool that allows us to gather important information about the environment in a cost-effective and efficient manner. As drone technology continues to advance, the potential applications and benefits of this technique are sure to grow, making it an exciting and rapidly-evolving field to watch in the coming years.

7.2 Equipment used in Drone Photogrammetry

Photogrammetry is a highly sophisticated field that requires the use of specialized equipment to capture, process, and analyze data. Drone photogrammetry is no different, and requires the use of a range of equipment to ensure that the results are accurate, reliable, and of high quality. In this chapter, we will explore some of the key equipment used in drone photogrammetry, including drones, cameras, GPS and IMU sensors, and software.

7.2.1 Drones

A drone, or unmanned aerial vehicle (UAV), is the most important piece of equipment in drone photogrammetry. Drones are equipped with cameras that capture images from the air, and they are capable of flying over areas that would otherwise be difficult or impossible to access. Drones come in various shapes and sizes, and each one is designed to meet specific needs and requirements. Some of the most popular drones used in photogrammetry are the DJI Phantom, Mavic, and Matrice series, as well as the Parrot Bebop and Anafi.

7.2.1.1 DJI Phantom Drones

Advantages:

1. Ease of use: DJI Phantom drones are designed for ease of use, with simple controls and intuitive flight modes. This makes it easy for new pilots to start flying right away.

2. Image Quality: The Phantom drones have cameras that produce high-quality images and videos, which are perfect for aerial photography and videography.

Disadvantages:

1. Price: DJI Phantom drones can be more expensive compared to other consumer drones on the market, which may make them less accessible to some users.

2. Size: The Phantom drones can be larger and bulkier compared to other consumer drones, which may make them less portable and harder to transport.

7.2.1.2 DJI Mavic Drones:

Advantages:

1. Portability: The Mavic drones are small and compact, making them easy to transport and store. They can be folded down for maximum portability.

2. Advanced Features: The Mavic drones have advanced features like obstacle avoidance, ActiveTrack, and TapFly, which make flying and capturing aerial footage easier and more enjoyable.

Disadvantages:

1. Range: The Mavic drones have a limited range compared to other DJI drones, which can be a drawback for users who need longer range capabilities.

2. Price: While more affordable than the Phantom drones, the Mavic drones can still be a bit expensive for some users.

7.2.1.3 DJI Matrice Drones

Advantages:

1. Durability: The Matrice drones are designed for commercial and industrial applications, with a durable build that can withstand tough conditions.

2. Customizability: The Matrice drones have multiple payload options and a modular design, allowing us Customizability: The Matrice

drones have multiple payload options and a modular design, allowing users to customize the drone for their specific needs.

Disadvantages:

1. Price: The Matrice drones are more expensive than other DJI drones, which can be a drawback for . users with limited budgets.
2. Complexity: The Matrice drones are designed for professional use and can be more complex to operate, which may make them less accessible for new pilots.

7.2.1.4 Parrot Bebop Drones

Advantages:

1. Price: The Parrot Bebop drones are more affordable compared to other high-end drones on the market, making them accessible to more users.
2. Ease of use: The Bebop drones are designed for ease of use, with simple controls and a user-friendly interface.

Disadvantages:

1. Image Quality: The Bebop drones have cameras that produce lower quality images and videos compared to other high-end drones, which can be a drawback for users who need high-quality aerial imagery
2. Range: The Bebop drones have limited range, which can be a drawback for users who need longer range capabilities.

7.2.1.5 Parrot Anafi Drones

Advantages:

1. Portability: The Anafi drones are small and lightweight, making them easy to transport and store.
2. Image Quality: The Anafi drones have cameras that produce high-quality images and videos, which are perfect for aerial photography and videography.

Disadvantages:

1. Price: While more affordable than some other high-end drones, the Anafi drones can still be a bit expensive for some users.
2. Limited Features: The Anafi drones have fewer advanced features compared to other high-end drones, which can be a drawback for users who need more control and functionality.

7.3 Cameras

The camera is the second most important piece of equipment in drone photogrammetry. A high-quality camera is essential to capturing images that are detailed, accurate, and of sufficient quality for photogrammetry purposes. Many drones are equipped with high-resolution cameras that are capable of capturing images with a high level of detail and accuracy. Some of the most popular cameras used in photogrammetry include the Sony RX1R II, Canon EOS 5DS R, and the Nikon D850. We will also discuss two alternatives with a more favorable price-quality ratio: the

Fujifilm X-T30 and Canon EOS Rebel T7i and one cheap alternative: Ricoh Theta Z1.

7.3.1.Sony RX1R II

Advantages:

1. Compact Size: The Sony RX1R II is a compact full-frame camera, making it easy to carry and travel with.

2. Image Quality: The camera features a high-resolution 42-megapixel sensor, delivering exceptional image quality and detail.

Disadvantages:

1. Price: The Sony RX1R II is a premium camera, with a relatively high price tag compared to other full-frame cameras.

2. Fixed Lens: The camera has a fixed 35mm lens, which can limit its versatility compared to cameras with interchangeable lenses.

7.3.2 Canon EOS 5DS R

Advantages:

1. High Resolution: The Canon EOS 5DS R has a 50-megapixel full-frame sensor, delivering high-resolution images.

2. Wide Range of Lenses: The camera is compatible with a wide range of Canon lenses, providing users with a variety of options for different shooting scenarios.

Disadvantages:

1. Price: The Canon EOS 5DS R is a high-end camera, with a relatively high price tag compared to other full-frame cameras.

2. Slow Continuous Shooting: The camera has a relatively slow continuous shooting rate compared to other full-frame cameras, which can be a drawback for fast-moving action.

7.3.3 Nikon D850

Advantages:

1. Versatility: The Nikon D850 is a versatile camera, with a 45-megapixel full-frame sensor and a wide range of capabilities, including high-speed continuous shooting, 4K video recording, and excellent low-light performance.

2. Durability: The camera is built to withstand tough conditions, making it a great choice for outdoor and adventure photography.

Disadvantages:

1. Price: The Nikon D850 is a premium camera, with a relatively high price tag compared to other full-frame cameras.

2. Complexity: The camera has a lot of features and controls, which can make it more complex for beginner photographers to navigate.

In general, all three cameras are high-end models that are ideal for professional photographers or serious hobbyists. The Sony RX1R II is a compact camera with exceptional image quality, the Canon EOS 5DS R has a high-resolution sensor and a wide range of lenses, and the Nikon D850 is a versatile and durable camera that can handle a variety of shooting scenarios.

But all these cameras are relatively expensive. Especially when you're starting with Drone Photogrammetry this can be an obstacle. Fortunately there are alternatives:

7.3.4 Fujifilm X-T30

Advantages:

1. Excellent Image Quality: The Fujifilm X-T30 has a 26.1 megapixel APS-C sensor that produces sharp and detailed images. The camera's X-Trans CMOS 4 sensor provides high-quality images with low noise, even in low-light conditions.

2. Compact and Lightweight: The Fujifilm X-T30 is a compact and lightweight camera, making it easy to carry around and use in various shooting scenarios. Despite its small size, the camera has a well-built and durable body.

Disadvantages:

1. Limited Battery Life: The Fujifilm X-T30 has a relatively small battery, which can limit the amount of time you can shoot without recharging or carrying extra batteries. The battery life is rated at approximately 380 shots per charge.

2. Limited Video Features: While the Fujifilm X-T30 is a great camera for still photography, its video capabilities are somewhat limited. It can shoot 4K video at 30 frames per second, but lacks some of the advanced video features found in other cameras.

7.3.5 Canon EOS Rebel T7i

Advantages:

1. User-Friendly Interface: The Canon EOS Rebel T7i is designed to be user-friendly, making it an excellent camera for beginners. It has an intuitive interface that is easy to navigate, with a variety of automatic shooting modes and built-in guides to help you get the best shot.

2. Good Autofocus System: The Canon EOS Rebel T7i has a fast and accurate autofocus system, with 45 autofocus points that cover most of the frame. This makes it easy to get sharp images, even in challenging lighting conditions.

Disadvantages:

1. Limited ISO Range: The Canon EOS Rebel T7i has a limited ISO range, which can make it challenging to shoot in low-light conditions without using a tripod or additional lighting. The maximum ISO setting is 25600, which may not be sufficient for some photographers.

2. Mediocre Battery Life: The Canon EOS Rebel T7i has a relatively short battery life, which may require you to carry extra batteries or limit your shooting time. The battery life is rated at approximately 600 shots per charge.

7.3.6 Ricoh Theta Z1

Advantages:

1. 360-Degree Capture: The Ricoh Theta Z1 is designed to capture 360-degree images, making it an excellent camera for virtual tours, real estate photography, and other applications where a full view of the scene is necessary. The camera captures both horizontal and vertical perspectives, which can provide a more immersive viewing experience.

2. High-Quality Images: The Ricoh Theta Z1 has dual 1-inch sensors and can capture 23-megapixel still images and 4K video. The camera also has built-in noise reduction and image stabilization, which can help to produce sharp and detailed images.

Disadvantages:

1. Limited Battery Life: The Ricoh Theta Z1 has a relatively short battery life, which can limit the amount of time you can shoot without recharging or carrying extra batteries. The battery life is rated at approximately 300 shots per charge.

2. Limited Post-Processing Options: The Ricoh Theta Z1 captures images in a specialized format that may require additional software to edit or convert. While the camera does have some built-in post-processing options, they are relatively limited compared to other cameras.

All of these cameras are suitable for drone photogrammetry and provide good value for their price. However, it's important to keep in mind that the best camera for drone photogrammetry will depend on the individual's specific needs and preferences, so it's a good idea to compare different models to see which one will work best for you.

7.4 GPS and IMU sensors

The use of GPS and IMU sensors in drone photogrammetry is essential to achieving high-quality results. These sensors work together to provide data that helps to accurately align images and create precise maps and models.

GPS sensors use satellite signals to determine the exact location of the drone in space. This information is critical for photogrammetry, as it helps to ensure that the images captured by the drone are correctly positioned and can be accurately processed. By providing data on the location of the drone, GPS sensors ensure that the images captured are aligned correctly and that the maps and models created are accurate and reliable.

IMU sensors, on the other hand, provide data on the orientation and motion of the drone. This information is used to correct for any movement or tilt of the drone during image capture. IMU sensors measure the drone's acceleration and orientation, allowing for real-time correction of any movement. This helps to ensure that the images captured are stable and free of any distortion.

When used together, GPS and IMU sensors provide a comprehensive data set that helps to ensure that the maps and models created by drone photogrammetry are of the highest quality. These sensors are an essential part of the drone photogrammetry process and play a critical role in achieving accurate and reliable results.

Drone technology has advanced greatly, and many drones now come equipped with integrated GPS and IMU sensors. This has made it easier than ever before to collect accurate data for photogrammetry purposes, and has opened up new opportunities for the use of drone photogrammetry in a wide range of applications, from surveying and mapping to environmental monitoring and emergency response.

7.4.1 Software

The final piece of equipment used in drone photogrammetry is software. We have already dealt with this subject in detail in an earlier chapter. Photogrammetry software is used to process the images captured by the drone and produce accurate, reliable maps and models. Some of the most popular photogrammetry software programs include Agisoft Photoscan, Pix4D, and DroneDeploy. These programs are designed to work with a wide range of images and data, including aerial images captured by UAVs.

7.5 Nowadays examples

Drone photogrammetry is being used in a wide range of industries, from agriculture to construction, and from environmental monitoring to disaster response. For example, in agriculture, drone photogrammetry is being used to monitor crop health, identify areas of stress, and optimize fertilizer and pesticide applications. In construction, it is being used to survey and map construction sites, monitor progress, and ensure that work is completed on time and within budget. In environmental monitoring, drone photogrammetry is being used to monitor the health of forests, track the movement of wildlife, and monitor the effects of climate change. In disaster response, it is being used to assess damage and respond to emergencies, such as earthquakes, hurricanes, and wildfires.

7.6 Conclusion

In conclusion, drone photogrammetry requires the use of specialized equipment to capture, process, and analyze data. The equipment used in drone photogrammetry includes drones, cameras, GPS and IMU sensors, and software. Each of these pieces of equipment plays an important role in ensuring that the results of drone photogrammetry are accurate, reliable, and of high quality. With the increasing use of drone photogrammetry in a wide range of industries, the equipment used in this field is becoming more sophisticated and capable of delivering even better results.

Chapter 8: Image Acquisition and Processing

Photogrammetry involves capturing images of a target area, and using these images to produce accurate and detailed maps and models. Drone photogrammetry involves capturing images using drones equipped with cameras, and then using specialized software to process these images into maps and models. In this chapter, we'll look at the steps involved in image acquisition and processing, and discuss some key factors that can impact the quality of the final results.

8.1.1 Image Acquisition

Image acquisition is the first step in drone photogrammetry. This involves flying the drone over the target area, and capturing images of the area from different angles and positions. To ensure accurate and reliable results, it is important to follow best practices for image acquisition, such as flying the drone in a grid pattern, and capturing images from multiple positions and angles.

The quality of the images captured by the drone will impact the quality of the final results, so it is important to use high-quality cameras that are capable of capturing clear and detailed images. Additionally, it is important to ensure that the images are captured in good lighting conditions, as poor lighting can lead to blurriness or other issues that can impact the quality of the final results.

8.1.2 Image Quality Assessment

Once the images have been captured, the next step is to assess the quality of the images. This involves evaluating the images to ensure that they are clear, detailed, and have sufficient overlap with other images. Overlap refers to the extent to which images overlap with each other, and is an important factor in determining the accuracy of the final results.

It is also important to assess the quality of the GPS and IMU data that was captured along with the images. This data is used to position and orient the images in 3D space, so it is important that it is accurate and reliable.

8.1.3 Image Processing

Once the images have been captured and assessed, the next step is to process the images using specialized software. This involves using software to stitch the images together, and create a 3D model of the target area. The software also uses the GPS and IMU data to position and orient the images in 3D space, and to correct any errors or inaccuracies in the data.

The quality of the final results will depend on a number of factors, including the quality of the images, the quality of the GPS and IMU data, and the accuracy of the processing software. Additionally, the complexity of the target area and the amount of detail that is required in the final results will also impact the quality of the final results.

8.2 Image rectification and georeferencing

One of the most critical stages of photogrammetry is image acquisition and processing, which involves the rectification and georeferencing of images.

Image rectification refers to the process of correcting image distortion caused by the camera lens, orientation, or terrain. This correction process ensures that the images are transformed into a standard coordinate system, making it easier to compare and merge images from different sources.

Georeferencing, on the other hand, involves assigning geographic coordinates to images, making it possible to integrate the images with other geospatial data, such as satellite imagery or digital maps. This process allows photogrammetrists to accurately align images with the ground and create a seamless mosaic of the study area.

Modern photogrammetry software, such as Autodesk ReCap Photo, Agisoft Photoscan, and DroneDeploy, make it possible to perform image rectification and georeferencing automatically. By utilizing GPS and IMU sensors, these programs can accurately determine the location and orientation of the camera during image capture.

An example of the benefits of image rectification and georeferencing can be seen in disaster response efforts. After a natural disaster such as an earthquake or hurricane, drones equipped with cameras can be quickly deployed to capture images of the affected area. By using image rectification and georeferencing, these images can be transformed into accurate and reliable maps, allowing emergency responders to quickly assess the extent of damage and plan their response.

In conclusion, image rectification and georeferencing are critical components of photogrammetry. By correcting image distortion and integrating images with geospatial data, photogrammetry provides a powerful tool for creating accurate and detailed maps, models, and information. Whether you are a geologist studying the formation of mountains, an archaeologist exploring ancient ruins, or an emergency responder assessing the impact of a natural disaster, photogrammetry provides the tools you need to better understand and analyze our world.

8.3 Image processing and stereo-plotting

Image acquisition and processing are crucial components of photogrammetry, as they determine the quality and accuracy of the final product. In this part, we will explore the important step of image processing and stereo-plotting in photogrammetry.

Stereo-plotting is the process of creating 3D information from two or more overlapping images. The overlapping images are combined to create a stereo-pair, which can then be viewed using a stereo-plotter. The stereo-plotter creates the illusion of depth by allowing the viewer to see the scene from two slightly different perspectives. By looking at the stereo-pair and adjusting the distance between the two images, the viewer can perceive the depth of objects in the scene. This information is then used to create a 3D model of the scene.

Stereo-plotting is a key component of photogrammetry because it allows the user to extract accurate 3D information from images. This information is used to create maps, models, and other products that are used in a wide range of applications. For example, stereo-plotting can be used to create topographic maps, digital terrain models, and orthorectified images. These products are used in fields such as surveying, engineering, agriculture, and environmental management.

Stereo-plotting is a highly specialized process that requires specialized software and equipment. The software used for stereo-plotting is often called a photogrammetric workstation. These workstations use complex algorithms to analyze the stereo-pair and extract the 3D information. Some of the most commonly used photogrammetric workstations include Pix4D, DroneDeploy, and Photoscanner.

One of the biggest advantages of stereo-plotting is its accuracy. Because the process involves creating a 3D model from overlapping images, the resulting product is highly accurate. This accuracy is particularly important for applications such as surveying, where even small errors can have significant impacts. In addition, stereo-plotting is a highly efficient process, as it allows users to create 3D models from large numbers of images quickly and easily.

Despite its many advantages, stereo-plotting is not without its limitations. One of the biggest limitations is the requirement for overlapping images. Without overlapping images, it is not possible to create a stereo-pair and perform stereo-plotting. Additionally, the process of stereo-plotting can be time-consuming and requires specialized software and equipment, which can be expensive.

Stereo-plotting is a critical component of photogrammetry that allows users to create accurate and efficient 3D models from images. While the process is not without its limitations, it is an important tool for a wide range of applications and is used by professionals in many fields. Whether you are a surveyor, an engineer, or simply someone who is interested in photogrammetry, understanding the basics of stereo-plotting is essential for success.

8.4 Digital terrain modeling and orthorectification

8.4.1 Digital Terrain Modeling

Digital terrain modeling is the process of creating a digital representation of the earth's surface. It involves using photogrammetric techniques to extract information about the topography of an area from aerial or satellite images. The resulting model provides a 3D representation of the area, including its elevation, slope, and aspect. This information is useful for a wide range of applications, including land use planning, natural resource management, disaster response and engineering design.

8.4.2 Orthorectification

Orthorectification is the process of correcting aerial or satellite images for the effects of topographic relief, atmospheric refraction and camera distortion. The result is an image that has been geometrically corrected so that the scale and position of features are accurate. Orthorectified images are essential for a wide range of photogrammetric applications, including digital terrain modeling, mapping and remote sensing.

Example:

A good example of the use of digital terrain modeling and orthorectification is in the field of environmental management. For instance, an environmental management organization might use a drone equipped with a high-resolution camera to capture images of a protected wilderness area. The images are then processed using photogrammetric techniques to create a digital terrain model and orthorectified images. The resulting information can be used to identify areas of land degradation, such as erosion, and to monitor changes in land use over time.

Another example is in the field of urban planning. City planners can use orthorectified aerial images to accurately measure the size and position of buildings, streets, and other features in a city. This information can be used to plan and design new developments, to assess the impact of new construction on the local environment, and to monitor changes in the urban landscape over time.

Digital terrain modeling and orthorectification are important steps in the image acquisition and processing stage of photogrammetry. They provide essential information for a wide range of applications, including land use planning, environmental management, and urban planning. With advances in technology, the use of drones and other aerial platforms, and the availability of high-resolution imagery, these techniques are becoming increasingly accessible and cost-effective.

8.4.3 Environmental monitoring and assessment

Photogrammetry and drone photogrammetry have become essential tools in environmental monitoring and assessment, providing valuable information about our planet's ecosystems and the impact of human activities on them. With the increasing availability of drones and photogrammetry software, it has become possible to gather large amounts of high-resolution data about the environment in a relatively short period of time. This data is crucial in understanding the impact of human activities on the environment and in developing strategies to protect it.

One example of the use of photogrammetry in environmental monitoring is the monitoring of deforestation. Deforestation has a significant impact on the environment, leading to soil erosion, loss of biodiversity, and an increase in greenhouse gas emissions. Photogrammetry can be used to monitor the extent of deforestation and to track changes over time. By analyzing satellite images or aerial photographs, scientists can identify the extent of deforestation, the areas that are most affected, and the impact of human activities on the environment.

Another example of the use of drone photogrammetry in environmental monitoring is the monitoring of wildlife populations. Drone photogrammetry can be used to count animals, such as whales and penguins, and to track their movements. This information is crucial in understanding the distribution and behavior of wildlife populations and in developing conservation strategies. For example, in Antarctica, drone photogrammetry has been used to monitor the distribution of penguin colonies and to track changes in their population size over time.

Another important application of photogrammetry in environmental monitoring is the assessment of the health of forests and other ecosystems. By analyzing the structure and composition of forests, scientists can understand the impact of human activities, such as logging, on the health of these ecosystems. Drone photogrammetry can be used to collect data about the height, density, and species composition of forests, providing valuable information for conservation and management purposes.

Photogrammetry and drone photogrammetry have become crucial tools in environmental monitoring and assessment, providing valuable data about the impact of human activities on the environment. Whether it is monitoring deforestation, wildlife populations, or the health of forests, photogrammetry has the potential to play a significant role in protecting and conserving our planet's ecosystems.

8.4.4 Cultural heritage and archaeology

Photogrammetry and drone photogrammetry have become increasingly popular in recent years for the study and preservation of cultural heritage and archaeology sites. These technologies allow for the creation of precise, three-dimensional models of heritage sites, which can be used for documentation, analysis, and interpretation. The use of drones provides a unique perspective that allows for the collection of detailed imagery from hard-to-reach locations.

One of the most appealing examples of photogrammetry in cultural heritage and archaeology is the use of drones to survey the ancient city of Palmyra, Syria. The city, which was once a thriving cultural center, was heavily damaged during the Syrian civil war. In 2016, archaeologists used drones to capture images of the site and create a three-dimensional model that allowed them to study the remaining structures and make plans for their preservation.

Another example of photogrammetry in cultural heritage is the use of drones to survey the historic city of Venice, Italy. The city, which is sinking into the water due to rising sea levels, is in need of preservation and protection. By using drones to survey the city, archaeologists and preservationists can create detailed maps of the city and its structures, which can then be used to make informed decisions about preservation efforts.

The use of drones in cultural heritage and archaeology also provides a unique perspective that allows researchers to view and study sites from different angles. This perspective can be used to uncover previously undiscovered structures, which can then be studied in more detail. For example, drones were used to survey the ancient city of Petra in Jordan, which allowed archaeologists to uncover previously unknown structures and make new discoveries about the city's history.

The use of photogrammetry and drone photogrammetry in cultural heritage and archaeology is providing a valuable tool for the preservation and study of our cultural heritage. By creating precise three-dimensional models of heritage sites, researchers can better understand and preserve these sites for future generations. As technology continues to evolve, we can expect to see even more exciting and innovative applications of photogrammetry and drone photogrammetry in this field.

8.4.5 Disaster management and emergency response

Disasters can strike at any time, and they often result in widespread damage to infrastructure, property, and lives. In these critical moments, fast and accurate information is crucial for effective response and recovery. This is where photogrammetry and drone photogrammetry play a vital role in disaster management and emergency response.

The use of aerial and drone-based photography to assess the extent of damage caused by natural and man-made disasters has become increasingly popular in recent years. This is because photogrammetry and drone photogrammetry provide a cost-effective, efficient, and quick way to acquire detailed and accurate information about the affected areas.

For example, after the devastating 2010 earthquake in Haiti, drone photogrammetry was used to survey the affected areas and provide information about the extent of damage. The images captured by drones were used to create high-resolution maps and 3D models, which helped aid organizations in their response and recovery efforts.

Another example is the use of drone photogrammetry in the aftermath of hurricanes, such as Hurricane Harvey in Texas in 2017. Drone imagery was used to assess the damage caused by the storm, which helped prioritize the allocation of resources and inform the recovery efforts.

In addition to disaster assessment, drone photogrammetry can also be used for search and rescue operations. Drones equipped with thermal cameras can quickly search large areas for missing persons, even in challenging terrains, such as forests and mountainous regions.

Photogrammetry and drone photogrammetry have proven to be powerful tools in disaster management and emergency response. They provide fast, efficient, and accurate information about the extent of damage caused by disasters, which helps aid organizations in their response and recovery efforts. As technology continues to advance, it is likely that these tools will become even more important in the years to come.

Chapter 9: Future Trends and Developments

Future Trends and Developments in Photogrammetry and Drone Photogrammetry

9.1 Advancements in Hardware and Software

Photogrammetry has come a long way since its inception, with advancements in technology driving the field to new heights. As we move forward, we can expect to see continued innovation in the hardware and software used for photogrammetry and drone photogrammetry. In this chapter, we will explore some of the exciting advancements in hardware and software that are shaping the future of this field.

9.2 Advancements in Drone Technology

Drones have revolutionized the way photogrammetry is performed, and this trend is only set to continue. The development of small, lightweight, and highly advanced drones has allowed for greater accessibility and ease of use for photogrammetrists. These drones are equipped with advanced cameras, GPS systems, and other sensors, providing high-quality and accurate data that can be used to generate precise maps, models, and other outputs.

Moreover, advancements in battery technology and drone design have made it possible to fly drones for longer periods of time, leading to the collection of more data, and more comprehensive maps. New drones are also being developed with foldable arms and compact designs, making them more portable and easier to transport to remote locations.

9.3 Software Innovations

The software used for photogrammetry and drone photogrammetry is also advancing at a rapid pace. Advancements in computer vision and artificial intelligence are enabling the development of software that can process large amounts of data and extract meaningful insights. For example, deep learning algorithms can be used to automatically detect and identify features in images, such as buildings, trees, and other landmarks.

Software is also being developed that can automate various stages of the photogrammetry process, including image rectification, georeferencing, and digital terrain modeling. This not only saves time and effort but also leads to more consistent and accurate results.

9.4 Augmented Reality and Virtual Reality

Augmented reality (AR) and virtual reality (VR) technologies are also being incorporated into photogrammetry and drone photogrammetry. AR and VR can be used to create interactive and immersive visualizations of maps, models, and other outputs, providing new and exciting ways to view and analyze data.

For example, AR and VR can be used to create 3D models of cultural heritage sites, allowing researchers and the public to virtually explore and interact with these sites, even if they are located far away or are in danger of being destroyed.

The future of photogrammetry and drone photogrammetry looks bright, with exciting advancements in hardware and software poised to transform the field in exciting ways. As technology continues to evolve, we can expect to see new and innovative applications emerge, and the capabilities of photogrammetry and drone photogrammetry will only continue to expand.

9.5 Integration with other technologies

Photogrammetry and drone photogrammetry are constantly evolving fields that are continuously shaped by advancements in technology. One of the most exciting trends in the industry is the integration of photogrammetry with other cutting-edge technologies. In this chapter, we'll explore some of the most promising examples of how photogrammetry and drone photogrammetry are being combined with other technologies to produce new and innovative solutions for various applications.

9.5.1 Virtual Reality (VR) and Augmented Reality (AR)

Virtual Reality (VR) and Augmented Reality (AR) are rapidly growing industries, and photogrammetry is playing an increasingly important role in their development. By integrating photogrammetry with VR and AR technologies, it is possible to create highly accurate and immersive virtual environments that can be used for a wide range of applications, from training and simulation to entertainment and gaming.

For example, VR and AR can be used in archaeology to create interactive 3D models of historical sites and ancient ruins, allowing people to explore and learn about these sites in a virtual environment. This type of technology can also be used in the restoration of cultural heritage sites, allowing architects and conservationists to explore and visualize their plans for the restoration process.

9.5.2 Building Information Modeling (BIM)

Building Information Modeling (BIM) is a digital representation of the physical and functional characteristics of a building, used in the design, construction, and maintenance of buildings. By integrating photogrammetry and drone photogrammetry with BIM, it is possible to create highly accurate 3D models of buildings that can be used for various purposes, such as construction planning, energy analysis, and facility management.

For example, a drone equipped with photogrammetry technology can be used to capture high-resolution images of a building. This data can then be processed using photogrammetry software to create a highly accurate 3D model of the building. This model can then be integrated with BIM software, allowing architects and engineers to visualize the building in a virtual environment, making it easier to identify design flaws, detect structural issues, and optimize energy efficiency.

9.5.3 Artificial Intelligence (AI)

Artificial Intelligence (AI) is rapidly advancing, and its integration with photogrammetry and drone photogrammetry is producing exciting new solutions for various applications. By combining photogrammetry with AI, it is possible to automate many of the processes involved in photogrammetry, from image acquisition and processing to data analysis and interpretation.

For example, AI can be used to automate the process of creating 3D models from aerial images captured by drones. This type of technology can be used in the agriculture sector to quickly and accurately assess crop yields and monitor the health of crops. It can also be used in urban areas to monitor changes in the built environment, such as the construction of new buildings or the demolition of old ones.

The integration of photogrammetry and drone photogrammetry with other technologies such as VR and AR, BIM, and AI is producing exciting new solutions for a wide range of applications. As technology continues to evolve, it is likely that we will see even more innovative and exciting developments in the field of photogrammetry and drone photogrammetry.

9.5.4 Emerging applications and industries

As the field of photogrammetry and drone photogrammetry continues to grow and evolve, it is important to take a look at the emerging applications and industries that are utilizing this technology to make a real impact. From construction and agriculture to media and entertainment, the potential uses for photogrammetry and drone photogrammetry are virtually limitless. In this chapter, we will explore some of the most exciting and innovative applications that are poised to shape the future of this field.

9.5.5 Construction and Infrastructure

One of the most exciting applications of photogrammetry and drone photogrammetry is in the construction and infrastructure industry. With the help of drones equipped with high-resolution cameras, construction companies are able to get a bird's-eye view of the construction site and get a better understanding of the lay of the land. This information can then be used to plan and design the construction project more accurately, reducing the potential for mistakes and increasing efficiency.

9.5.6 Agriculture

Another growing industry that is utilizing photogrammetry and drone photogrammetry is agriculture. With drones equipped with specialized sensors, farmers are able to get an in-depth look at their crops and fields, allowing them to monitor crop health and make more informed decisions about irrigation, fertilization, and pest management. This technology has the potential to revolutionize the way that agriculture is done, making it more efficient and sustainable.

9.5.7 Media and Entertainment

Photogrammetry and drone photogrammetry are also making a big impact in the media and entertainment industries. With the ability to capture stunning aerial footage, filmmakers and photographers are now able to get unique perspectives and angles that were previously impossible to achieve. This technology has already been used in a number of blockbuster movies, including "The Hobbit" and "Star Wars," and is sure to play a big role in the future of film and television production.

As we have seen, the field of photogrammetry and drone photogrammetry is rapidly evolving and has the potential to make a real impact in a number of different industries. Whether it is construction, agriculture, media and entertainment, or something else entirely, the future of photogrammetry and drone photogrammetry is sure to be exciting and full of new opportunities.

9.6 Ethical and legal considerations

Photogrammetry and drone photogrammetry have revolutionized the way that we collect and analyze data, allowing us to gather detailed information about the world around us in new and exciting ways.

However, as these technologies continue to advance, it is important that we consider the ethical and legal implications of their use.

One of the most significant ethical considerations related to photogrammetry and drone photogrammetry is privacy. Drones equipped with high-resolution cameras are capable of capturing detailed images of private property, which could potentially be used for nefarious purposes. For this reason, it is important that we establish clear regulations and guidelines for the use of drones in populated areas, in order to protect the privacy of individuals.

Another important ethical consideration is safety. As drones become more widespread and more advanced, there is a risk that they could collide with other aircraft or cause damage to property. It is therefore important that we establish regulations to ensure that drones are operated safely and responsibly, in order to minimize the risk of accidents.

Legal considerations are also an important factor to consider when it comes to photogrammetry and drone photogrammetry. For example, in many countries, there are laws in place that regulate the use of drones and the collection of data by remote sensing technologies. In some cases, these laws are still evolving, as regulators work to keep pace with the rapid advancements in these technologies.

Despite these ethical and legal considerations, there is no denying the tremendous potential of photogrammetry and drone photogrammetry to benefit society in a multitude of ways. As these technologies continue to advance, we are likely to see an increased adoption in new industries and applications, and an expanded ability to gather and analyze data on a scale that was previously impossible.

To give an example, in the field of archaeology, drones equipped with high-resolution cameras and photogrammetry software can be used to create detailed, 3D models of historical sites and ancient ruins, providing new insights into the past and allowing archaeologists to study these sites in new and exciting ways.

As we look to the future of photogrammetry and drone photogrammetry, it is important that we continue to consider the ethical and legal implications of these technologies, in order to ensure that they are used in ways that are responsible and benefit society as a whole. By doing so, we can help to ensure that these exciting and rapidly-evolving technologies continue to have a positive impact on the world for generations to come.

Chapter 10: Conclusion

Photogrammetry and Drone Photogrammetry are two branches of remote sensing that have been revolutionizing the way we collect, process, and analyze spatial data. Over the years, these techniques have proven to be invaluable in numerous fields and industries, from mapping and surveying to cultural heritage and archaeology, environmental monitoring and assessment, and disaster management and emergency response. The development of new hardware and software technologies has also made it possible to collect and process data more efficiently and accurately, opening up new avenues for research and innovation.

In this book, we have provided a comprehensive overview of photogrammetry and drone photogrammetry, exploring the key concepts and techniques involved in collecting, processing, and analyzing spatial data. We have looked at the various applications of these techniques, including mapping and surveying, environmental monitoring and assessment, cultural heritage and archaeology, and disaster management and emergency response, and discussed some of the most exciting and innovative trends and developments in these fields.

Looking ahead, there is no doubt that photogrammetry and drone photogrammetry will continue to play a major role in shaping our world and improving our understanding of it. The integration of photogrammetry with other technologies, such as artificial intelligence and machine learning, will enable us to process and analyze data faster and more accurately, helping us to tackle some of the biggest challenges facing our planet.

Despite these exciting developments, there are also important ethical and legal considerations that need to be taken into account. As the use of photogrammetry and drone photogrammetry continues to grow, it is crucial that we ensure that the data we collect and the insights we gain are used responsibly and ethically.

In conclusion, photogrammetry and drone photogrammetry are powerful and versatile techniques that offer limitless possibilities for exploring and understanding our world. Whether you are an aspiring photogrammetrist, a seasoned professional, or simply someone with a passion for technology and innovation, there is no doubt that this field offers endless opportunities for growth and discovery.

We hope that this book has provided you with a solid foundation in photogrammetry and drone photogrammetry and has inspired you to explore these fascinating and dynamic fields further. Whether you decide to delve deeper into the technical details, or focus more on the applications and trends, there is no limit to what you can achieve. So don't be afraid to take the next step and start your journey into the world of photogrammetry and drone photogrammetry today!